Dear parents, grandparents, teachers and frie...

This book is an informative representation of l... about 1,000 years ago. Through its story children... life as it may have been: the cultu... lifestyle, government and socio-economic structure. Activities provi... children with an opportunity to become involved in the process of creative learning.

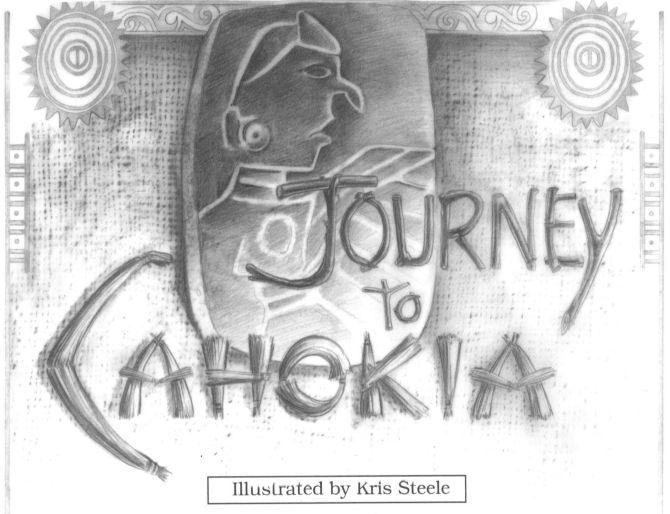

Illustrated by Kris Steele

Technical Assistance by William Iseminger

CMMS Advisory Committee: Doris Marti, Chairperson, Marilyn Gass, Zennie Herring, Ettus Hiatt, Judy Horton, William Iseminger, Jan Lowis, Christine Pallozola

Produced by American Educational Press in cooperation with Cahokia Mounds Museum Society

4113 N. Longview

Phoenix, Arizona 85014

P.O. Box 382

Collinsville, Illinois 62234

Copyright © 1995 by Cahokia Mounds Museum Society

ISBN# 1-881563-02-2   Library of Congress # 95-070899   CIP

All rights reserved. Reproduction of activities including pages 24-30 is permissible for use in the classroom only.

Reproduction of these materials for an entire school system is strictly prohibited.

At the top of this page is a sketch of the **Birdman Tablet**, found during excavations on Monks Mound. It has become the symbol of Cahokia Mounds.

No one is sure exactly when or how the first people came to live in America.

However, scientists believe the first people traveled across a land bridge connecting Alaska and Siberia. During the last Ice Age, possibly more than 20,000 to 40,000 years ago, the land bridge formed when the sea levels were low.

The people moved about in small family groups. They followed herds of caribou, mammoths and other large animals, reaching the Midwest as early as 11,000 years ago. Many changes occurred over thousands of years. For example, the climate warmed, the large animals died out, and smaller animals and edible plants became more abundant. These changes led to new ways of living for the people.

As time passed, the descendants of these early people settled throughout North and South America.

A **culture** emerged thousands of years later throughout the Central and Southeastern United States. **Archaeologists** call it the **Mississippian Culture**. Some of these people settled in the fertile valley known as the American Bottom in southwestern Illinois. We do not know what they called themselves. There are no written records of these people.

Yet we know many things about the **prehistoric** Mississippian Culture from archaeologists and other American Indians. For example, the people grew many crops. Corn was the most important food in their diet.

Mississippian people built permanent structures such as temples and earthen mounds. They developed an organized way of life with complex government, religious and social systems. The Mississippian people traded with many others from faraway places.

By **A. D.** 1000, about one thousand years ago, a great city formed as a center of the Mississippian Culture. The city covered over 5 square miles, included more than 120 mounds and had an estimated population of 20,000 by A. D. 1150.

By A.D. 1400 the city had been abandoned. In the 1800s it was named **Cahokia** for a later Indian group that lived in the area.

Join Running Deer and his father as they leave their small Mississippian village to journey to Cahokia. Through their story you can imagine life as it may have been one thousand years ago.

Running Deer lived with his family in a small village. He knew every building in the village and how it was used. The council lodge and open-air house were used by family clan members for community meetings. As he passed the elevated **granary** building, he saw that it was filled with corn and knew they had a good harvest.

Running Deer's mother was near the granary preparing a deer skin by scraping it with a **chert** scraper. He knew how important the deer was to his people. Deer meat was his favorite food. All parts of the deer were used. The brains were rubbed into hides to keep them soft and the antlers were used for tools and ornaments. Tools such as pins, needles and **awls** were made from the bones. His mother would boil down the hooves to make glue. She planned to make clothing or bedding from the skin she was preparing.

Tomorrow Running Deer would go with his father, Stands Tall, to Cahokia, which was one day's journey away. He wondered what the great City of the Sun, Cahokia, would be like. His father had often described its magnificent temples and mounds. Father was a trader who often traveled to faraway places, but this would be his son's first trip. Running Deer was eager to see the great city and to visit his cousin and grandmother who lived there.

At daybreak everyone said good-bye to Stands Tall and his son as they began their journey along the well-worn footpath leading to Cahokia.

As they walked they saw women gathering nuts in the distance. During the year they also worked to collect the seeds, persimmons, mulberries, paw paw, blackberries, roots, grapes and herbs which were very important to their diet.

Stands Tall remembered when he passed this field in the spring and saw women and children using antler rakes and stone hoes. They were preparing the soil and planting crops to feed the leaders, their families and clan members. Now the field was covered with corn, pumpkins, squash, gourds, Jerusalem artichokes and sunflowers. They also grew many other seed-bearing plants, such as lamb's quarter, May grass and little barley. Today the women were gathering food to store for the winter.

Father waved to hunters carrying a deer back to their village. Someday, Running Deer thought, he too would leave the village before dawn with the men to hunt animals such as deer, bear, rabbit, turkey, duck, muskrat, raccoon and squirrel. All the meat, fur, feathers and bones would be used by the people. Besides hunting, men also made tools.

When the sun was high over head, they turned off the main footpath toward the creek and the village on its banks. This was Running Deer's first visit to the small fishing community.

Running Deer was surprised to see such a small village with so few people. This was nothing like his village, which was home to several hundred people, or the city of Cahokia, which was home to nearly 20,000 people!

Stands Tall came to trade with the fishermen of the village. He **bartered** fishing tools, such as bone hooks and harpoon points, for fresh fish.

Running Deer helped the men and boys fish with nets while his father traded. The sun was hot but the cool water moving past his legs was refreshing. He liked the feeling of mud squishing between his toes as he moved about in the water. The fishermen caught suckers, catfish, sunfish and bass. The men gave Running Deer a fish for helping them.

Stands Tall and Running Deer approached a man hollowing a log to make a canoe. The canoe maker first spread burning coals on the log to char the wood. Then he moved the coals and scraped away the charred area with chert and mussel shell tools. This process was repeated many times until the log was hollowed out to the proper depth. The outside was shaped with a chert **adze**.

Several dugout canoes lined the shore nearby. Stands Tall spoke with the man about a new canoe for his next trading journey. He would travel creeks and rivers to trade in far away towns and villages.

As Stands Tall and his son continued their trip, the path followed a creek in the direction of Cahokia. In the distance Running Deer could see the tall mounds of Cahokia for the first time. Father, who had been there many, many times, told him about the great city and its people.

"Cahokia has magnificent earthen mounds. It is the grandest city of our people," Stands Tall told him. "It also has a large wall (**stockade**) which encloses the center of the city. There are neighborhoods where groups of families live and plazas for games, markets and ceremonies. Cahokia is a very crowded city."

"The chief and his advisors are the highest class. Next in importance are the **nobles**, such as your uncle. Nobles supervise construction and agriculture. Traders like me follow in line of position and importance. Commoners, such as farmers, workers and craftsmen, have the lowest status. They work the fields, build the structures and make goods for the upper classes, " he continued. "Some highly skilled craftsmen can advance in position."

When Stands Tall and his son passed a large ridgetop mound, they knew they had reached the edge of the city of Cahokia. The path led them through the neighborhoods of the commoners before they arrived at the home of Stands Tall's brother. Uncle was a noble and lived near the wall. His son, Wild Crane, greeted the travelers as they approached.

The sun was setting but Running Deer was anxious to see the city. His cousin took him to the great stockade which surrounded the inner city of Cahokia. "The wall has recently been rebuilt," Wild Crane explained. "It is so long that 20,000 trees had to be cut for it." Running Deer had never seen such a huge wall. It was built of log posts and stood above the ground twice as tall as his father. From a nearby watch tower (**bastion**) a guard kept an eye on the boys.

Running Deer was eager to see the great chief, his priests and other nobles who lived inside the wall. He would have to wait until the next day to see the great homes surrounding the **plaza** and those built high up on the flat-top mounds.

That night, Running Deer was so excited he had difficulty falling asleep. He tossed and turned as he anticipated what he would see and do the next day.

Early the next morning the cousins began exploring Wild Crane's neighborhood. They saw a few men enter the **sweat lodge**, a low, round building covered with mats. Inside, the men sprinkled water on hot rocks until steam filled the lodge. The boys knew this special building was used by the men to cleanse their bodies and spirits.

Next the boys stopped to help a group of relatives build a new house. They helped place the wooden poles into a deep trench. When all the poles were in place, the boys helped fill the trench with dirt.

Some poles were lashed together with **cordage**, or twine, especially where roof timbers joined the walls. Young trees, or **saplings** (**wattle**), were woven like a basket around posts, forming a strong wall. It would be plastered with a clay mixture (**daub**) or covered with mats.

The roof would be covered with thatch (bundles of grass). The bundles would be placed in overlapping rows to help keep the inside of the house dry.

Some people in the neighborhood were preparing materials for the afternoon market. The cousins stopped to watch the **flintknapper**. He explained to them how natural stone materials, such as sandstone, granite and chert (**flint**), were made into stone tools.

The boys watched the flintknapper strike the chert at just the right angle with stone and deer antler tools. This made small pieces flake away. Some of the small pieces would be used for **arrowpoints** and scrapers. Running Deer wondered if he could ever learn to make such finely notched arrowpoints.

The boys saw the many **knives**, drills, picks, adzes, **axes** and **hoes** the flintknapper was preparing to take to market.

Running Deer and his cousin stopped to watch their relatives prepare corn (**maize**). One woman was shelling dried kernels from corn cobs. Another was grinding dry corn into meal with a mano and metate (grinding tools made of stone or wood). The corn meal could be mixed with water, shaped into flat, thin cakes and baked.

Some of the dry corn would be soaked in lyewater to remove the tough skins. The tender kernels would then be washed thoroughly, boiled in water and eaten as hominy.

Some corn was placed into baskets, clay pots and wooden bowls for storage. The surplus corn would be used for trade.

Wild Crane's mother was parching corn in a pot over the fire. She stirred it until the kernels popped open.

"I like the parched corn my mother makes for my father to eat on his trips," Running Deer commented, "but I like corn best in the summer when the kernels are soft. Mother removes the silks, rewraps the ear in its husks and soaks it in water. Then she roasts it in hot coals and I eat it."

In another area of the city, the boys stopped to watch the construction of a new **flat-top (platform) mound**. Wild Crane pointed to the long line of workers carrying baskets of dirt on their backs to the mound.

He had learned much about mound building from his father who is a supervisor. "Different kinds of dirt are used in mound construction to help with water drainage and to prevent erosion," he told his cousin.

"Some of the older mounds are quite large now. Once they were much smaller," Wild Crane explained. "When a noble died he was buried in a **roundtop (conical)** or **ridgetop mound**. Then his home on a flat-top mound was burned. More dirt was added to cover it and make a larger mound for his successor. Then they built a new home on top. My father says that the great mound has been enlarged at least 8 times."

That afternoon Stands Tall took the boys through the L-shaped gate in the stockade and into the Central Plaza of Cahokia.

Running Deer was excited as he passed through the gate. He stopped in amazement upon entering the plaza. Before them were mounds and buildings in every direction!

The majority of mounds they saw were flat-top mounds. Dwellings for the elite leaders as well as temples, council lodges and **charnel** buildings were constructed on these platform mounds. Stands Tall told them that the tall building on top of the largest mound (now called **Monks Mound**) was the main temple and home of the chief. He also said that only very important people could go up the log steps on the front of the mound.

CONICAL MOUND

The conical mounds (roundtop) were often used as burial places for the **elite** classes, such as chiefs and nobles. One large conical mound stood across the plaza opposite the mound of the Great Chief. Running Deer wondered what important leader was buried in it.

There were only a few ridgetop mounds built at Cahokia. These mounds were used to mark important locations and were sometimes used for special burials. One small ridgetop mound was in the plaza and Running Deer wondered why it was built there.

There was so much to learn about this great city.

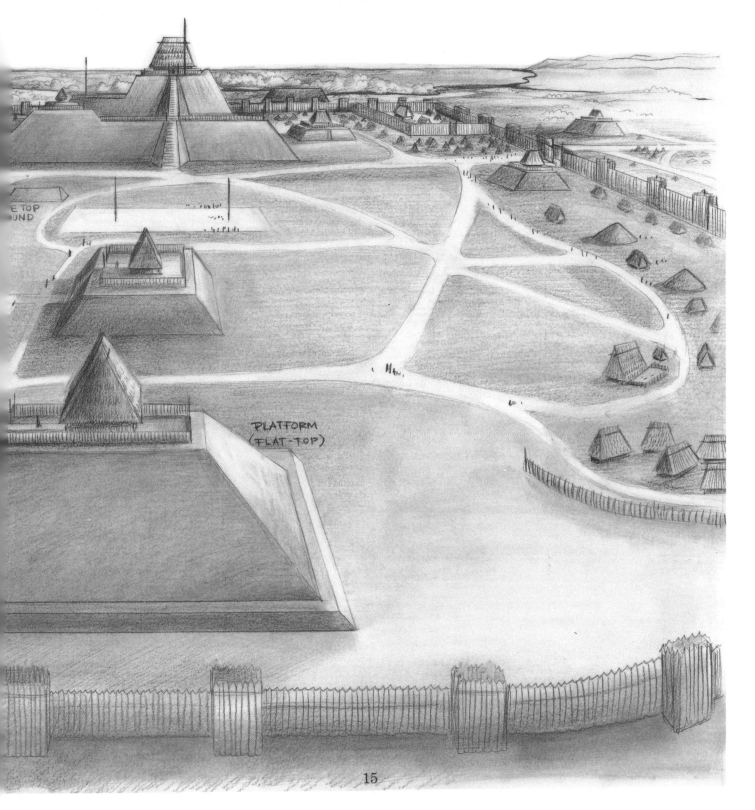

PLATFORM
(FLAT-TOP)

One area of the plaza was a vast marketplace. The cousins passed rows and rows of traders as they made their way through the crowd. They were amazed by the variety of pots, mats, baskets, moccasins, tools and jewelry they saw. There were many kinds of food, too.

Running Deer saw, for the first time, **mica** ornaments from the mountains of the East and copper jewelry from the lakes of the North. A trader showed them the huge shells from the great sea to the south and the many kinds of beads, pendants and cups made from them. He told them about the great sea with water as far as he could see. The boys could not imagine that.

The trader held up a beautiful shell pendant (**gorget**) for everyone to see. It glowed in the sunlight. Stands Tall offered to trade salt for the shell pendant. The trader accepted and both men were pleased with the barter.

The boys passed people trading wooden bowls, herb medicines, clothing and items such as bowls, rattles and combs made from turtle shell.

Running Deer and his cousin stopped next to watch a woman display her pottery. The boys seemed curious so she carefully explained how she made her pottery.

"I collect clay from stream beds and remove the small rocks. Then, I dry the clay," she said. "I add burned, crushed mussel shell for strength. Then I add water and knead the mixture. Next, I make large rolls of clay and coil them atop one another. I smooth them together with my fingers and tools of shell and gourd rind to get the shape I want," she said. "Then I make a design in the damp clay vessel and let it dry for several weeks. Finally, I fire it in an open pit."

That evening Grandmother told stories of this great city to the children.

One was a story her great-grandfather told her about an early leader who was buried in a small ridgetop mound just south of the stockade. The leader was placed on a blanket of shell beads. Valuable pieces of mica and a rolled copper staff were buried with him. Hundreds of arrows were buried there also. Their fine points of stone had come from places that were many days travel away. When the great leader died many people were sacrificed to go with him.

The boys listened eagerly. One day they would tell these same stories to their children's children.

Before the cousins went to bed Grandmother presented a shell, beaded necklace to Running Deer in honor of his first visit to Cahokia. He fell asleep thinking of all he had seen and heard and wondering what tomorrow would bring.

Early the next morning Stands Tall and the boys followed the crowd to the sun calendar, a great circle of tall posts (now called **Woodhenge**). Thousands of people had gathered to watch the sun rise to mark the beginning of the Harvest Festival. They were thankful for an abundant harvest.

On this day (the fall **equinox**) the sun emerges from behind Monks Mound and lines up with certain poles on the circle. Everyone watched as the sun slowly appeared. Then the people began to sing and chant. They were led by a sun priest who was perched on a post in the center of the circle.

In the distance, the Great Chief stood in front of his home on Monks Mound to greet the sun. All the people of Cahokia believed the Great Chief to be the brother of the Sun, who was their principal god.

After the sunrise ceremony Stands Tall and the boys followed the happy crowd back to the stockade, through the gates and into the center of the city. The boys were excited as they moved towards the plaza.

In the plaza, crowds of people were celebrating. They were wearing their finest clothes. Lines of dancers moved to the rhythm of music made with drums, flutes and rattles.

Many had their bodies painted with designs and symbols. A falcon dancer had his face painted with a forked-eye design. Father explained that Running Deer could identify people of high status by the tattoos on their bodies. Bone needles dipped in colored pigment such as **ochre** (red and yellow), **hematite** (red) and carbon (black) were used to tattoo designs on the elite.

"I like the falcon dancer best," Running Deer declared to his cousin, "because he looks like a bird and a man."

The boys watched many games being played by men and women. Some played a shell guessing game, while others played dice games. These were games of chance. Many different games used dice made from plum pits, bones, **sticks**, pieces of cane or broken pottery. Dice were marked on one side with either designs or colors. They were tossed into the air and caught in a basket. Players received points depending upon how the dice landed.

Some men played stickball. A leather ball stuffed with deer hair was tossed into play at the center of the field. The players used sticks made with netted hoops on the ends to catch the ball. The object was to carry or throw the ball across the field through the opposite team's goal. Each goal scored a point. The game was rough and there was much betting.

Still others held ring-and-pin contests, attempting to catch hollow bones on a string with the tip of a pointed stick. Some players were very skilled in flipping the bones and catching them on the sticks. Running Deer had practiced this game many times. In his village he was one of the best players.

The boys waited for the most popular event to begin—the game of **chunkey**. The idea of the game was to throw a spear at a moving target. It was played by two men. One player would roll a polished stone disc. Both players would run along and throw their spears where they thought the stone would stop rolling. The player whose spear was closest scored the points.

Today there would be contests all day to determine who was the best player. Men, including leaders, had traveled many days from all directions to compete in the games. Each one hoped to be the champion player. The cousins watched as the contest began.

At the end of the day's festivities, the Great Chief honored the winner of the chunkey contest. The tattooed chief was dressed in his ceremonial attire—a magnificent beaded and feathered cape, a feather headdress, a fine shell and copper necklace and the largest **earspools** Running Deer had ever seen!

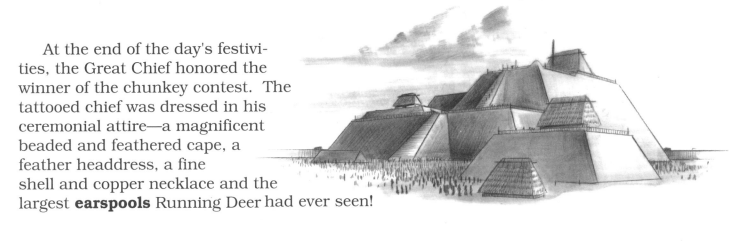

Thousands of people watched as the winner slowly approached the Great Chief. As the champion knelt before him, the Great Chief awarded him an engraved shell pendant. Running Deer watched in awe. He would always remember this exciting day in the City of the Sun.

The sun was setting as Stands Tall and the boys left the plaza. Tomorrow Running Deer must say good-bye to Grandmother and to Wild Crane and return to his village with his father.

Someday, when he grew up, Running Deer promised he would return and compete in the chunkey games. Maybe he too would be the champion in the Harvest Festival contest. Until then he would practice—and dream of winning.

Cattail Doll

In the historic period (and probably in Mississippian times) dolls and toys were made for Indian children from the dried leaves of the cattail plant. Below are directions for creating your own traditional cattail doll. Corn husks can be substituted for cattails.

Directions: Soak cattails until soft. (1) Stack 6 or 8 leaves on top of each other with the rounded side up. (2) Bend in middle and (3) tie with string about 1 1/4" to 1 1/2" from the bend for head.

(4) Below head on each side, pull up 1 or 2 cattails (depending on thickness) and (5) bend for arms. Bring the extra length down to the sides. (6) Tie arms at the top and criss-cross the string across the back to hold ends.

(7) Tie a string about 2" below arms for the waist. Divide cattails in half and tie at the "ankles" for a boy or pull out cattails into a fan-shape for a girl. Allow to dry.

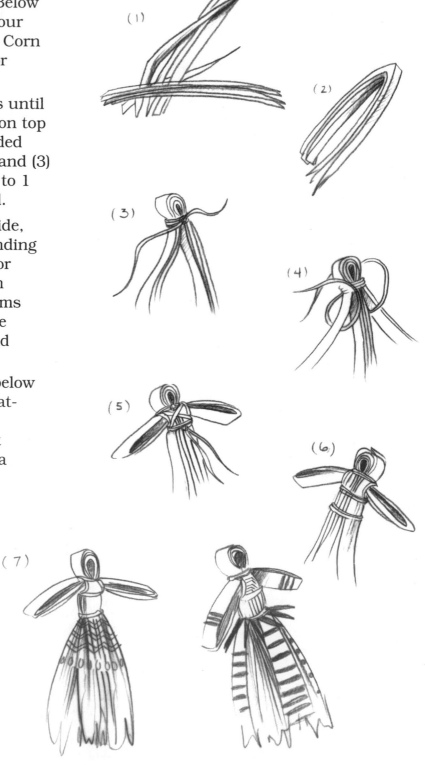

Crossword puzzle

Complete the crossword puzzle below. Fill in the spaces with the correct word from the definitions listed below.

Across

3. Roundtop mound used for burials.
4. Worn as a necklace or pendant.
7. Bundles of grass used to cover roofs.
9. Another name for a defensive wall.
11. Guard tower built along the stockade.
13. Makes tools and weapons of stone.
14. Saplings wound around wall posts in buildings.
15. Another name for corn.
16. First day of spring and fall.
18. Another name for flint.
19. Young tree used for building.
20. The upper social class of Cahokia.
21. Mound used as a marker.

Down

1. Largest mound at Cahokia is called_____Mound.
2. A red-colored mineral used in paints.
5. A building used to prepare dead bodies for burial.
6. Mixture of wet clay and grass, plastered over wattle.
8. Another name for a flat-top mound.
10. Center of the Mississippian Culture.
11. Sandstone tablet with design of eagle dancer is called the_____Tablet.
12. An early Indian civilization found in Central and Southeastern U.S. is _____Culture.
17. A red or yellow mineral used in paints.

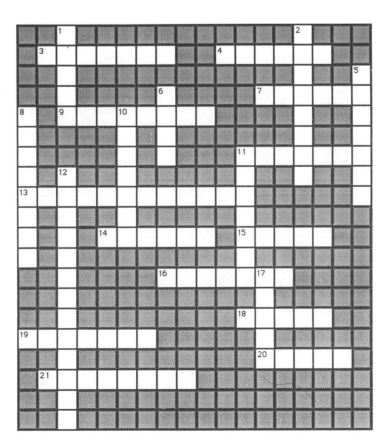

Mask Making

Items needed: piece of canvas or leather (or heavy brown paper), styrofoam head used for wigs, pins, paints, scissors and white glue.

Directions: Cut brown paper to desired shape and size. Cut openings for eyes, nose and mouth. Paint or color decorations onto mask. Paste stick to base of mask to hold in front of face.

or

Cut out piece of canvas or leather to desired size. Soak leather in water until soft. Cover face of styrofoam head with leather and pin in place. If using canvas, first cover styrofoam head with wax paper. Next, cover both sides of canvas with glue and place over styrofoam head to form shape. Pin in place. Allow material to dry completely. Remove from form. Cut openings for eyes, nose and mouth. Paint decorations.

"THE SUN"

"FALCON FORKED EYE"

"FALCON WEEPING EYE"

EARTH
"THE FOUR DIRECTIONS"

26

Burden Baskets

Burden Baskets were carried on the back with a strap that fit across the forehead. Backpacks are modern versions of burden baskets. You can make a burden basket by simply following the directions below.

Items needed: 2 plain brown paper grocery bags, wide masking tape, scissors, stapler, one strip of cloth (approximately 1" wide x 2' long), paint, paintbrush, markers or crayons.

1. Place one grocery bag inside the other.

2. Cut off 3" from the top of the bags.

3. Tape the top edges of the bags together with wide masking tape. Half the tape goes on the inside edge and half on the outside edge of the bags.

4. Decorate the bags with paints, markers and/or crayons to look like a woven basket. You can decorate the cloth strips, too.

5. Staple the cloth strip to the top edge of the basket. Strip must fit your head. Gather lightweight objects for your basket and enjoy.

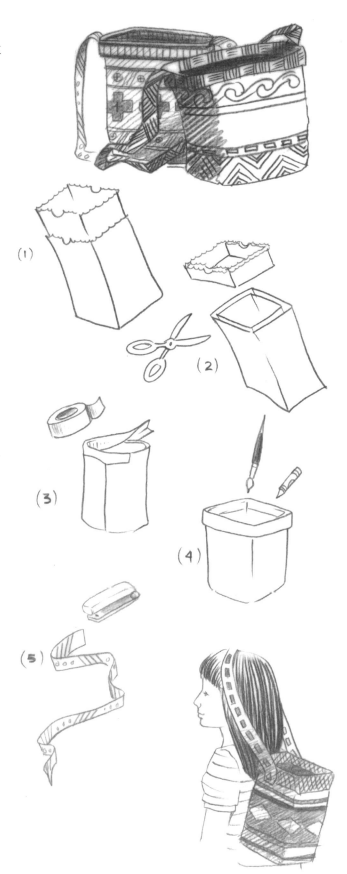

Matching Game

Draw a line from the word to the correct picture.

granary

hoe

Birdman Tablet

sweatlodge

sticks used in dice game

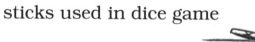

Cahokia arrowpoint

chunkey stones

earspools

stone knife

gorget

Make a Mound

Monks Mound has a volume of 22 million cubic feet, or 14,666,666 baskets full of dirt. Each basket held about 1.5 cubic feet or 55 pounds of dirt. If 30 students each filled 8 baskets of earth a day, it would take 167 years to build Monks Mound! However, it was actually built in several stages over a 300-year period by many people. Digging sticks and hoes were used to loosen the dirt which was then placed in baskets. The baskets of dirt were taken to the mound and dumped, then workers packed it with their feet.

Make a mound. Copy this page. You may enlarge it if you wish. Cut out shapes and trace onto green construction paper or posterboard. Fold along dotted lines as shown to make conical, platform and ridgetop mounds. See if you can construct a city like Cahokia.

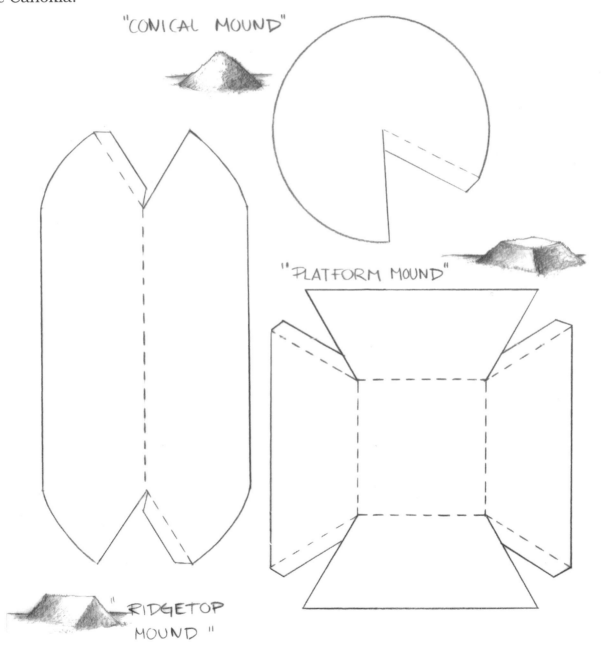

"CONICAL MOUND"

"PLATFORM MOUND"

"RIDGETOP MOUND"

Color a Gorget

To make your own gorget necklace, copy the chunkey player gorget picture below. Color it using your choice of colors. Cut out the dark circles at the top of the gorget and string yarn through the holes. Tie and enjoy.

Cahokia Today

You can step back in time when you visit Cahokia Mounds today. The 2,200 acre Cahokia Mounds State Historic Site has preserved 68 of the original 120 mounds! You can walk to the top of the ten-story high Monks Mound or view it and the site of the Central Plaza from the huge window in the Interpretive Center. Beautiful bronze panels, displaying human and bird figures, the Stockade and Monks Mound, greet you at the entrance doors.

You can see what life may have been like 1,000 years ago as you walk through a re-creation of a Cahokian neighborhood after viewing the award-winning multimedia show. Life-size models portray the daily activities of the Mississippian Culture. In the exhibit islands you can see the artifacts they made, the structures they built and the customs and beliefs they practiced.

Solstice and equinox sunrise observances are held at the reconstructed Woodhenge sun calendar, self-guided tours are available year-round and guided tours are offered seasonally. Activities and programs include Heritage America (a Native American festival), Kids' Day, Native Harvest Festival, Winter Lecture Series, storytelling programs, archaeological field schools, nature/culture hikes and much more. Contact the site for more information or a Calendar of Events.

Cahokia Mounds State Historic Site

~~P.O. Box 681~~ 30 RAMEY STREET

Collinsville, IL 62234

618-346-5160

Glossary and Answer Page

A.D.—stands for the Latin term "Anno Domini" (the year of the Lord).

Adze—an axe-like tool used to peel bark off trees and carve wood. It was made with a stone blade placed at a right angle to the handle.

Archaeologist—a person who collects and studies the artifacts of the past and attempts to explain people's way of life from this evidence.

Awl—a pointed tool for making holes in wood or leather, usually made from bone.

Barter—to trade goods or services without the exchange of money.

Bastion—a guard tower built along the stockade wall.

Birdman Tablet—a sandstone tablet engraved with the design of an eagle dancer.

Charnel house—a building where a dead body is prepared for burial.

Chert—a kind of rock, also known as flint, used to make tools and weapons.

Cordage—ropes or twine made of plant fibers.

Culture—the way of life led by a group of people, including all their knowledge, customs, beliefs, rules and things they made.

Equinox—when the sun rises due east, marking the first day of spring or first day of fall, and day and night are the same length.

Flint—a very hard stone which can be shaped by chipping (knapping) into sharp-edged cutting tools and arrowpoints.

Flintknapper—a craftsman who makes tools and weapons out of stone.

Granary—a building for storing corn or other food products.

Hematite—a red mineral that is crushed into a powder to make paint.

Mica—a shiny mineral that separates into thin layers and is used for jewelry.

Mississippian Culture—an Indian culture that was found throughout the Southeast and Mississippi Valley.

Monks Mound—the largest mound at Cahokia. It is 100 feet high and covers 14 acres.

Noble—a person of high social rank.

Ochre—a red or yellow mineral crushed into a powder to make paint.

Plaza—an open courtyard surrounded by buildings and other structures.

Prehistoric—the period before a written history.

Stockade—stout posts set to form a defensive wall, like a fort.

Woodhenge—a great circle of posts used as a sun calendar.

Crossword Answers

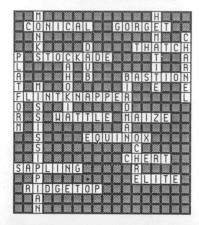

Matching Game

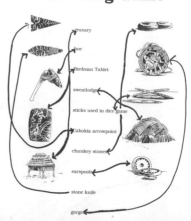

granary
hoe
Birdman Tablet
sweatlodge
sticks used in dice game
Cahokia arrowpoint
chunkey stone
earspool
stone knife
gorget

32